Handwriting Without Tears®
by Learning Without Tears

the Handwriting Interactive Teaching Tool™
hitt.LWTears.com/ext/CH/2018
More details are on the back cover.

P9-AET-102

Name: *oliva*

Cursive Handwriting

pianist   *teacher*   *singer*

8001 MacArthur Blvd
Cabin John, MD 20818
LWTears.com | 888.983.8409

Author: Jan Z. Olsen, OTR
Content Advisors: Christina Bretz, OTR/L, Tania Ferrandino, OTR/L
Illustrators: Jan Z. Olsen, OTR, Julie Koborg
Graphic Designers: Carol Johnston, Julie Koborg
Editors: Annie Cassidy, Megan Parker

Copyright © 2018 Learning Without Tears
Ninth Edition
ISBN: 978-1-939814-48-7
3456789PAH222120
Printed in the USA

January 2, 2018

Dear Student,

Can you read this?
It's cursive. Your teacher will help you learn to read and write cursive. I hope that you enjoy the book.

Sincerely,
Jan Z. Olsen

Aa Bb Cc Dd Ee Ff Gg Hh Ii Jj Kk Ll Mm
9 50 8 10 20 24 12 14 32 34 38 22 60

TABLE OF CONTENTS

Lowercase Letters
Magic c Letters

Lowercase: h t p

Lowercase: e l f

Lowercase: u y i j

Lowercase: k r s

Tow Truck Letters: o w b v

Capitals

Writing Activities

Cursive Lowercase

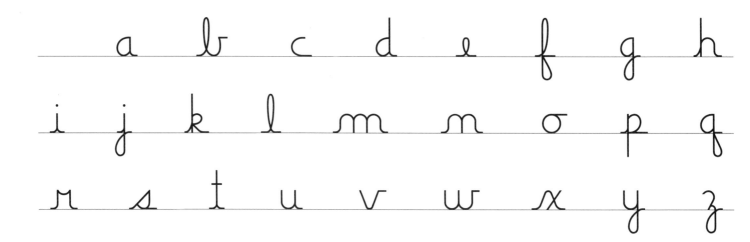

Connection Rule: When two letters are connected, the first letter is the "boss" of the connection.

1. Base line connections: If the first letter ends on the base line (22 letters), start the next letter on the base line.
2. High connections: If the first letter ends high (Tow Truck Letters: o, w, b, v), start the next letter high.

Cursive Capitals

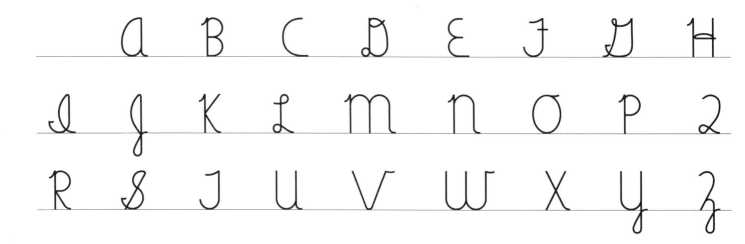

Connection Rule: Capitals do not have to connect.

1. Connect if it's easy; the capital ends on the base line and on the right side.
2. Don't connect if it's tricky, a high ending, or wrong side.

Cursive Warm-Ups

Under and over	Up and straight down	Up and loop down	Descending loop

Start on the star. Do one row a day.

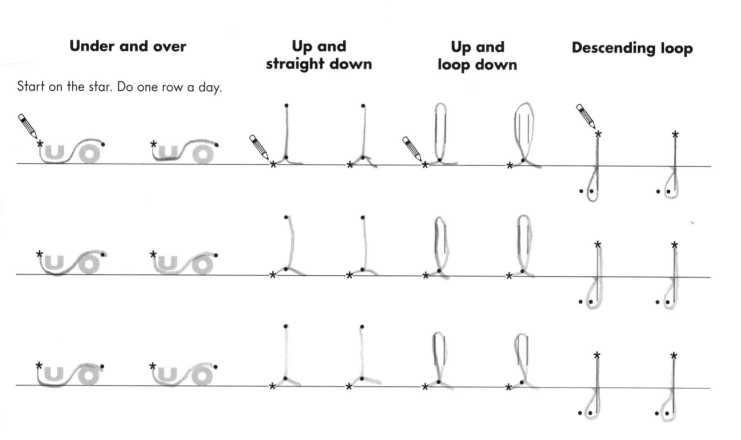

My Name in Cursive

Name: olivia

Name: olivia

Paper Placement & Pencil Skills

LEFT-HANDED
Place the **left** corner higher.

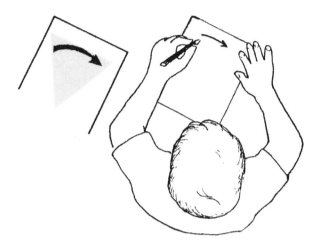

RIGHT-HANDED
Place the **right** corner higher.

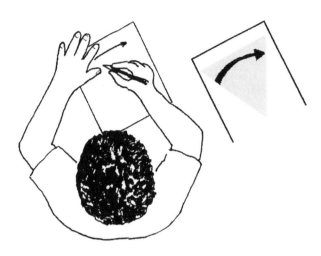

Standard grip: Hold pencil with **thumb + index finger.** Pencil rests on middle finger.

Eraser points to **left** shoulder.

Eraser points to **right** shoulder.

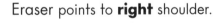

Alternate grip: Hold pencil with **thumb + index and middle fingers.** Pencil rests on ring finger.

Learn & Check

Learn letters, words, sentences, and how to check them.
When you see the box ☐, it's time to check your work.

☑ **Check letter** Teachers: Help children ☑ their letter for correct start, steps, and bump.

1. Start correctly.

2. Do each step.

3. Bump the lines.

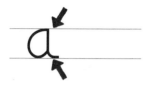

☑ **Check word** Teachers: Help children ☑ their word for correct letter size, placement, and Connections.

1. Make letters the correct size.
2. Place letters correctly: tall, small, or descending.

3. Connect letters correctly.

Tall   **Small**   **Descending**

☑ **Check sentence** Teachers: Help children ☑ their sentence for correct capitalization, word spacing, and ending punctuation.

1. Start with a capital.   **2.** Put space between words.   **3.** End with **.** **?** or **!**

c is C

Hi! I'm the Magic C Bunny. I'll help you start cursive.

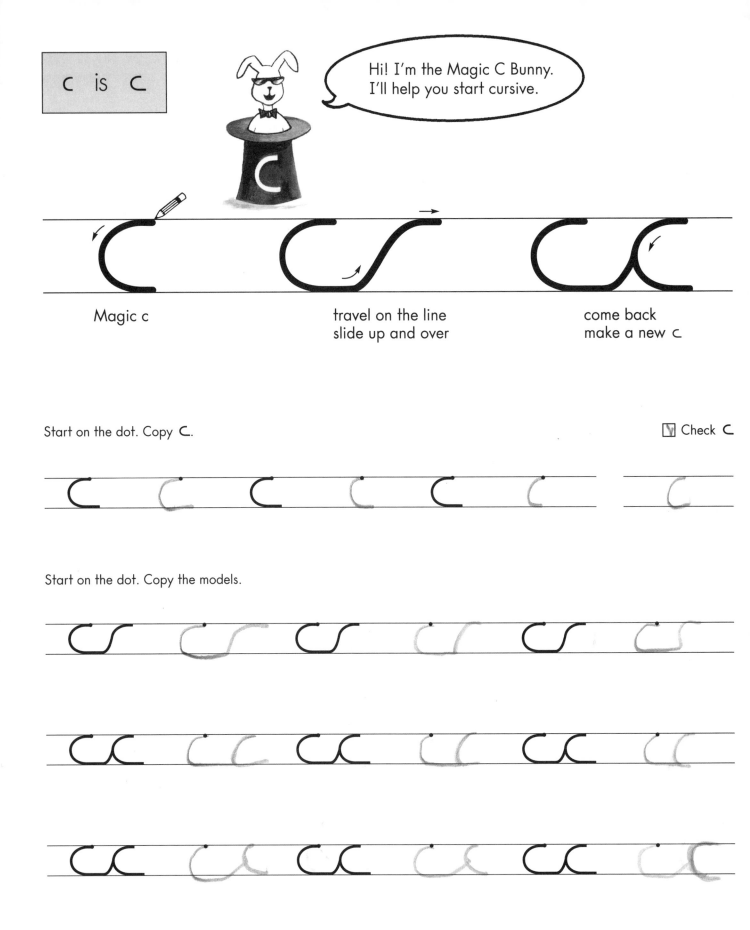

Magic c

travel on the line
slide up and over

come back
make a new c

Start on the dot. Copy C.

☑ Check C

Start on the dot. Copy the models.

☑ Check letter.   Teachers: Help children ✓ their letter for correct start, steps, and bumps.

8   *Cursive Handwriting*   © 2018 Learning Without Tears

a is a

Change c into a. Here's how:

bump

Magic c

up like a

back down
bump
travel away

Start on the dot. Copy a.

☑ Check a

a a a a a a a

Start on the dot. Copy the models.

ar a ar a ar a

ac ac ac ac ac ac

ca ca ca ca ca ca

d	is	d

Now change c into d.

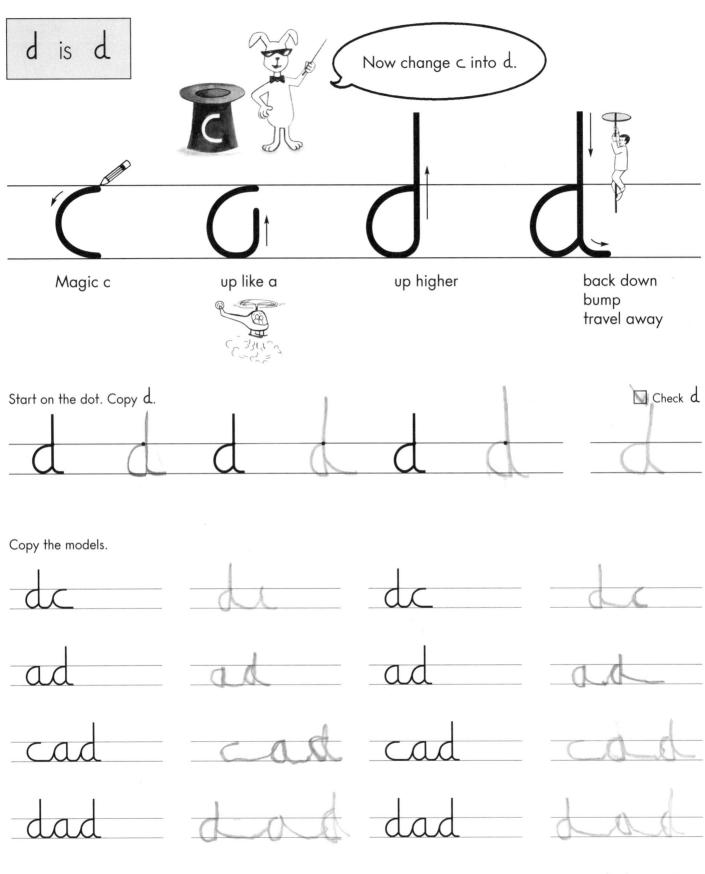

Magic c

up like a

up higher

back down
bump
travel away

Start on the dot. Copy d.

☑ Check d

Copy the models.

dc   dc   dc   dc

ad   ad   ad   ad

cad   cad   cad   cad

dad   dad   dad   dad

☑ Check dad

☑ Check word.   Teachers: Help children ✔ their word for correct letter size, placement, and connections.

© 2018 Learning Without Tears

Copy d.

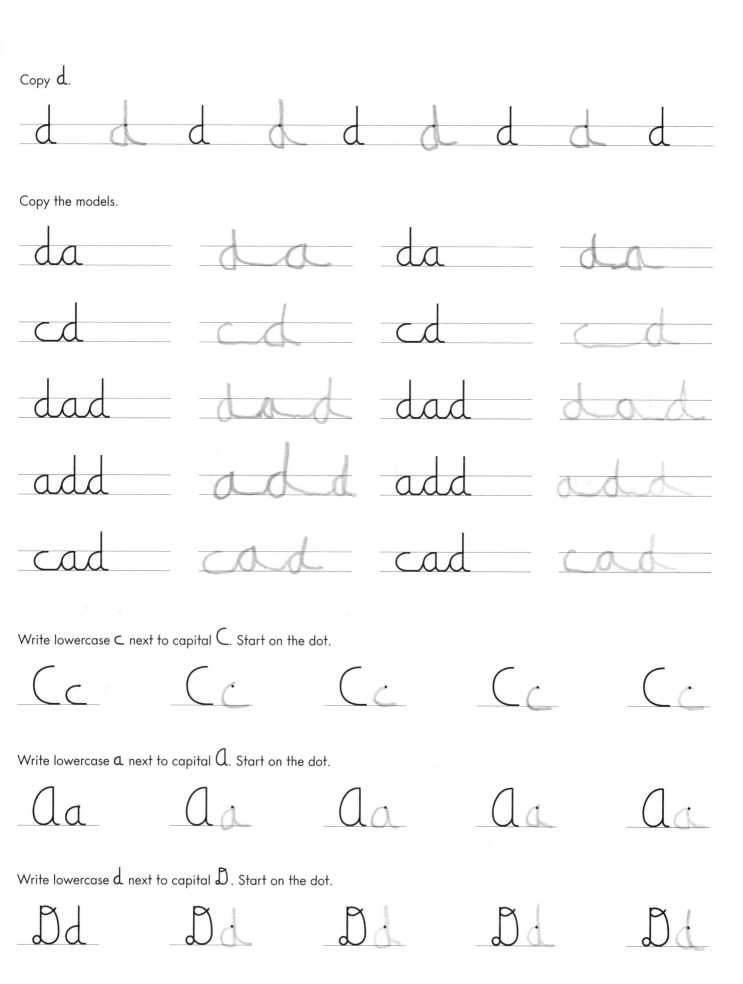

Copy the models.

da da da da

cd cd cd cd

dad dad dad dad

add add add add

cad cad cad cad

Write lowercase c next to capital C. Start on the dot.

Cc Cc Cc Cc Cc

Write lowercase a next to capital A. Start on the dot.

Aa Aa Aa Aa Aa

Write lowercase d next to capital D. Start on the dot.

Dd Dd Dd Dd Dd

g is _g_

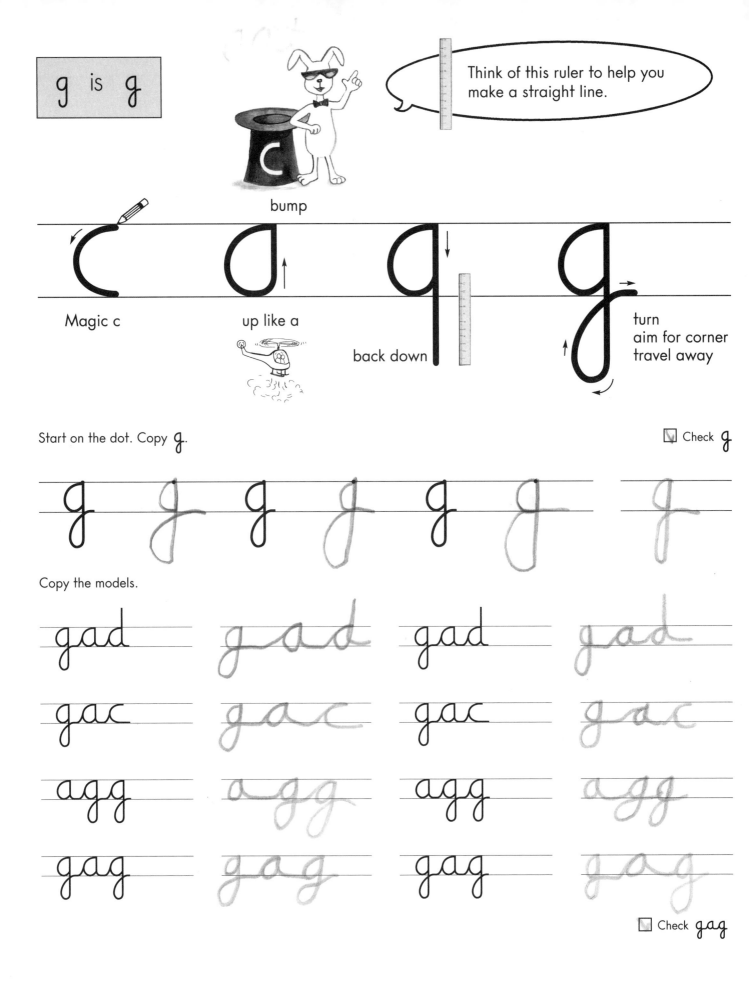

bump

Think of this ruler to help you make a straight line.

Magic c

up like a

back down

turn
aim for corner
travel away

Start on the dot. Copy _g_.

☐ Check _g_

g   g   g   g   g   g   f

Copy the models.

gad   gad   gad   gad

gac   gac   gac   gac

agg   agg   agg   agg

gag   gag   gag   gag

☐ Check _gag_

Copy g.

Copy the models.

Write lowercase g next to capital 𝒢. Start on the dot.

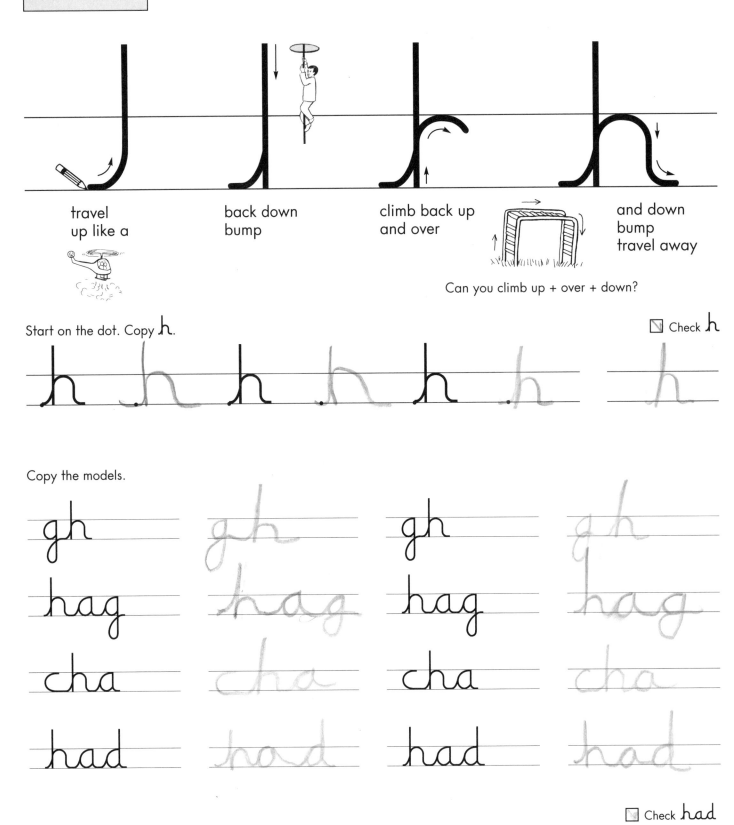

h is h

travel
up like a

back down
bump

climb back up
and over

and down
bump
travel away

Can you climb up + over + down?

Start on the dot. Copy h.

☒ Check h

h h h h h h h

Copy the models.

gh   gh   gh   gh

hag   hag   hag   hag

cha   cha   cha   cha

had   had   had   had

☐ Check had

Copy h.

h h h h h h h h h h

Copy the models.

ha   ha   ha   ha

ah   ah   ah   ah

had   had   had   had

cha   cha   cha   cha

hag   hag   hag   hag

hac   hac   hac   hac

aha   aha   aha   aha

Write lowercase h next to capital H. Start on the dot.

Hh   Hh   Hh   Hh   Hh

t is t

Left-handed?
You may cross this way.

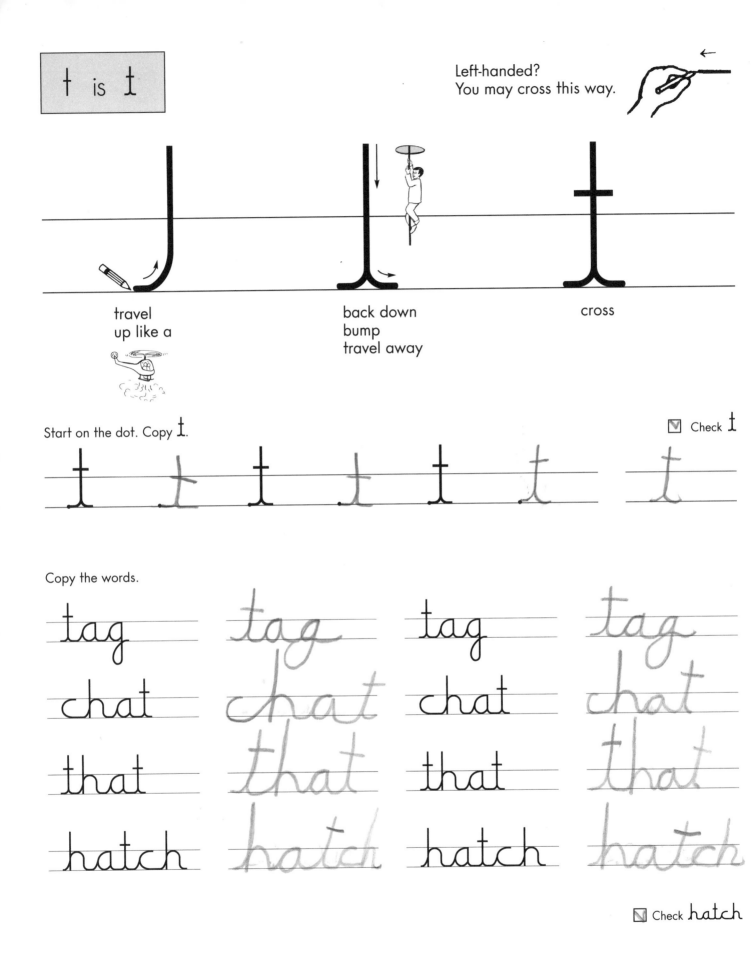

travel
up like a

back down
bump
travel away

cross

Start on the dot. Copy t.   ☑ Check t

t   t   t   t   t   t   t

Copy the words.

tag   tag   tag   tag

chat   chat   chat   chat

that   that   that   that

hatch   hatch   hatch   hatch

☑ Check hatch

Copy t.

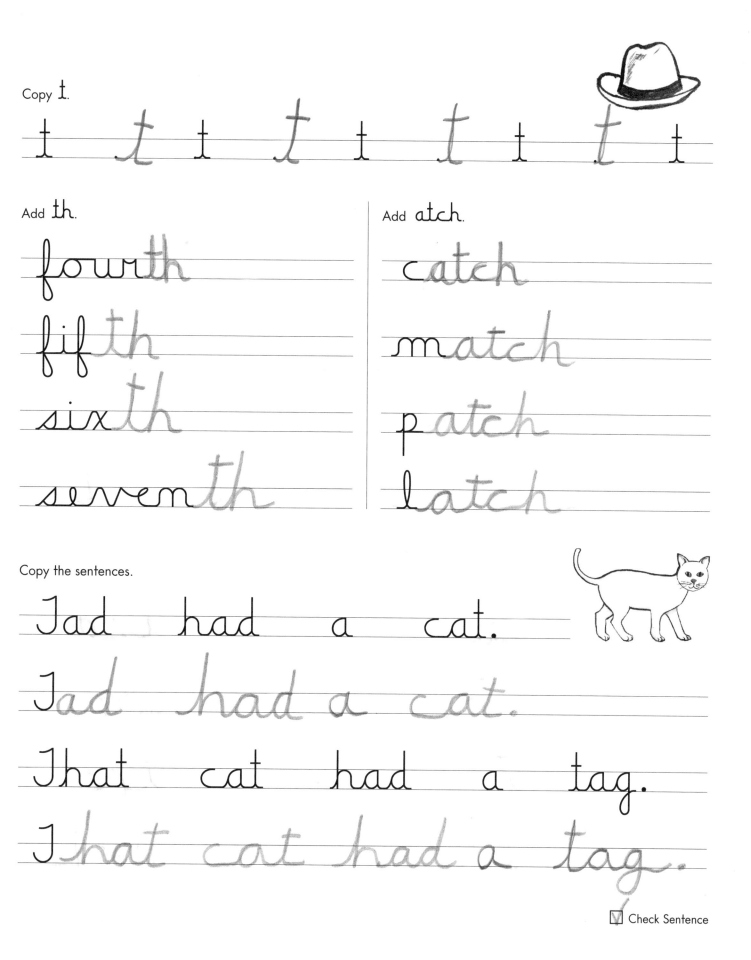

t t t t t t t t

Add th.

fourth
fifth
sixth
seventh

Add atch.

catch
match
patch
latch

Copy the sentences.

Tad had a cat.
Tad had a cat.
That cat had a tag.
That cat had a tag.

☑ Check Sentence

☑ Check sentence.   Teachers: Help children ✔ their sentence for correct capitalization, word spacing, and ending punctuation.

Cursive Handwriting   **17**

p	is	℘

Be sure to stay on the pole when you climb back up.

bump

travel
up

back down

climb back up
and over
and around

bump
travel away

Start on the dot. Copy ℘.

☐ Check ℘

℘ · ℘ · ℘ · ℘ · ℘ · ℘ · ℘

Copy the words.

pad   pad   pad   pad

tap   tap   tap   tap

patch   patch   patch   patch

chap   chap   chap   chap

☐ Check chap

Copy p.

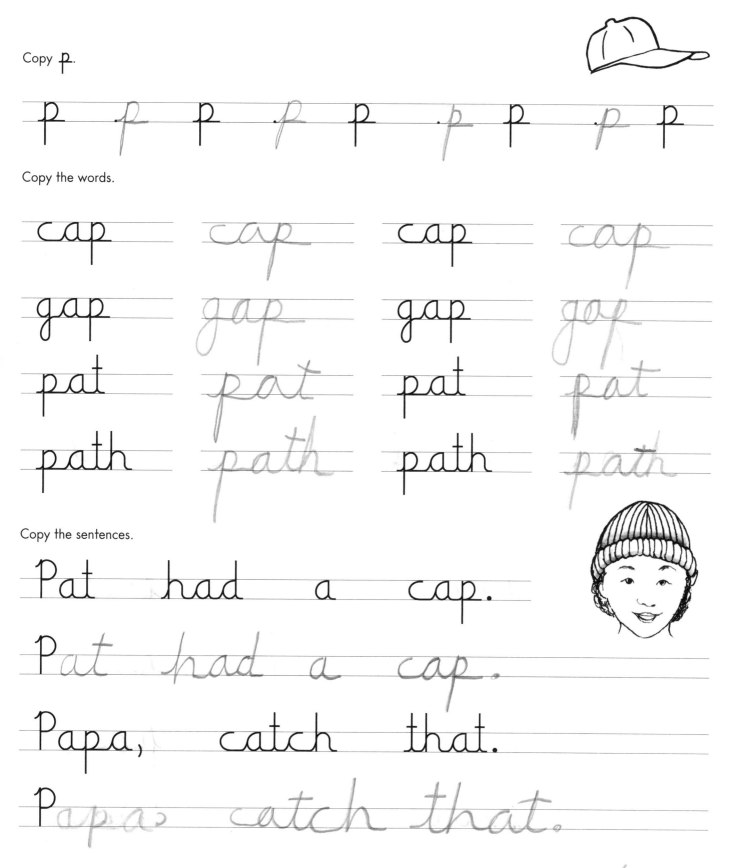

p   p   p   p   p   p   p   p   p   p   p   p

Copy the words.

cap   cap   cap   cap

gap   gap   gap   gap

pat   pat   pat   pat

path   path   path   path

Copy the sentences.

Pat had a cap.

Pat had a cap.

Papa, catch that.

Papa, catch that.

☑ Check Sentence

Name that letter! It's ___ e ___.

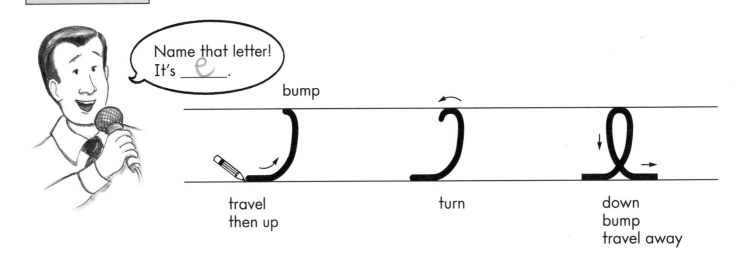

bump

travel
then up

turn

down
bump
travel away

Start on the dot. Copy l.   ☐ Check l

l   l   l   l   l   l   l

Copy the words.

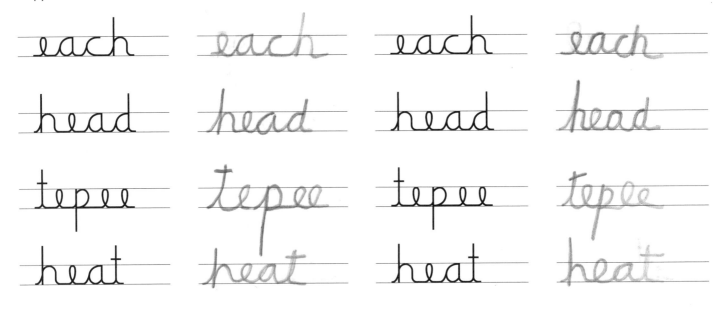

each   each   each   each

head   head   head   head

tepee   tepee   tepee   tepee

heat   heat   heat   heat

☑ Check heat

Copy .

l   l   l   l   l   l   l   l   l

Add *ace*.

race

place

lace

face

Add *ape*.

shape

grape

cape

tape

Add *eep*.

deep

jeep

sleep

keep

Copy the sentences.

Ed   ate   the   peach.

Ed   ate   the   peach.

Ed   patched   the   cage.

Ed   patched   the   cage.

☑ Check Sentence

l is ℓ

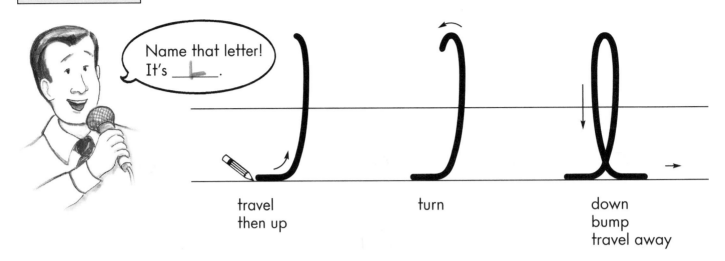

Name that letter!
It's ____ .

travel
then up

turn

down
bump
travel away

Start on the dot. Copy ℓ.

☑ Check ℓ

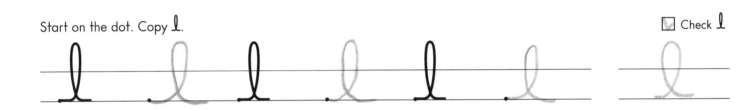

Copy the words.

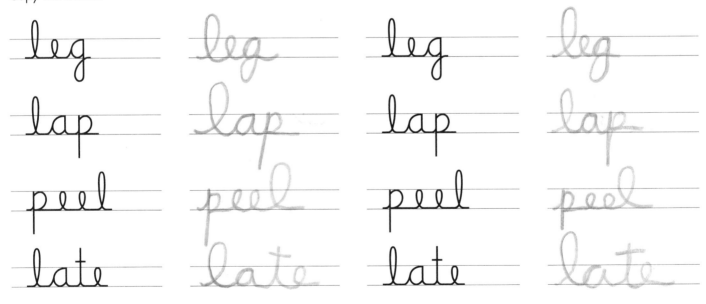

leg   leg   leg   leg

lap   lap   lap   lap

peel   peel   peel   peel

late   late   late   late

☑ Check late

Copy *l*.

l l l l l l l l l l l

Add *all*.

hall

mall

fall

tall

Add *ple*.

purple

sample

simple

apple

Add *eel*.

wheel

peel

feel

heel

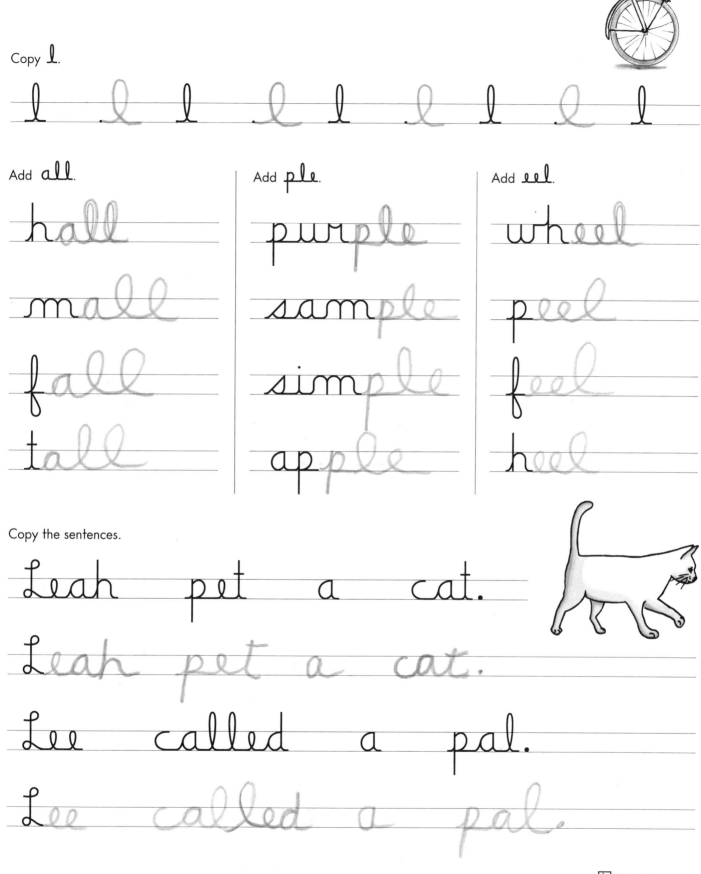

Copy the sentences.

Leah pet a cat.

Leah pet a cat.

Lee called a pal.

Lee called a pal.

☑ Check Sentence

f is f

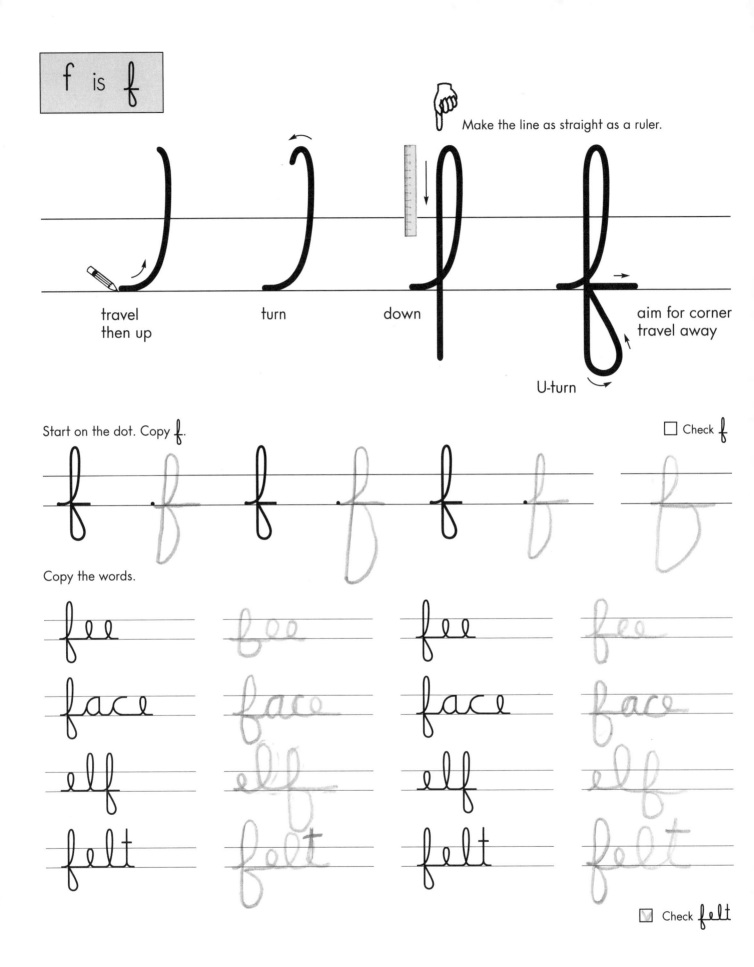

Make the line as straight as a ruler.

travel
then up

turn

down

aim for corner
travel away

U-turn

Start on the dot. Copy f.

☐ Check f

Copy the words.

fee   fee   fee   fee

face   face   face   face

elf   elf   elf   elf

felt   felt   felt   felt

☑ Check felt

Copy f.

f f f f f f f f

Add ift.

lift

gift

shift

drift

Add fle.

waffle

raffle

sniffle

duffle

Copy the sentences.

Fala felt the eel.

Fala felt the eel.

Face that fact.

Face that fact.

☐ Check Sentence

a b c d e f g h i j k l m
n o p q r s t u v w x y z

Wait for the teacher to play The Freeze Game.

each - peach

each - peach

hat - that

hat - that

fall - tall

fall - tall

led - fled

led - fled

lace - place

lace - place

age - page

age - page

ate - gate

ate - gate

ace - face

ace - face

See teacher's guide.

cap, c-a-p

eat → eat

Here are irregular verbs.
Translate the verbs to cursive.

Wait for the teacher to spell the words.
Write the Silly Spelling Words in cursive.

1. eat   eat   1. eat

2. ate   ate   2. ate

3. fall   fall   3. fall

4. fell

5. lead

6. led

7. feel

8. felt

u is u

Ride the u.
Then back down.

bump

down
travel up

back down
bump
travel away

Start on the dot. Copy u.   ☐ Check u

u   •   u   •   u   •   _____

Copy the words.

up   _____   up   _____

glue   _____   glue   _____

clue   _____   clue   _____

cut   _____   cut   _____

☐ Check cut

Copy u.

u   u   u   u   u

Add ful.

careful   hope

cheer   help

peace   harm

use   color

Copy the sentences.

Ulla laughed at that.

U

Ulla caught a cap.

U

☐ Check Sentence

y	is	y

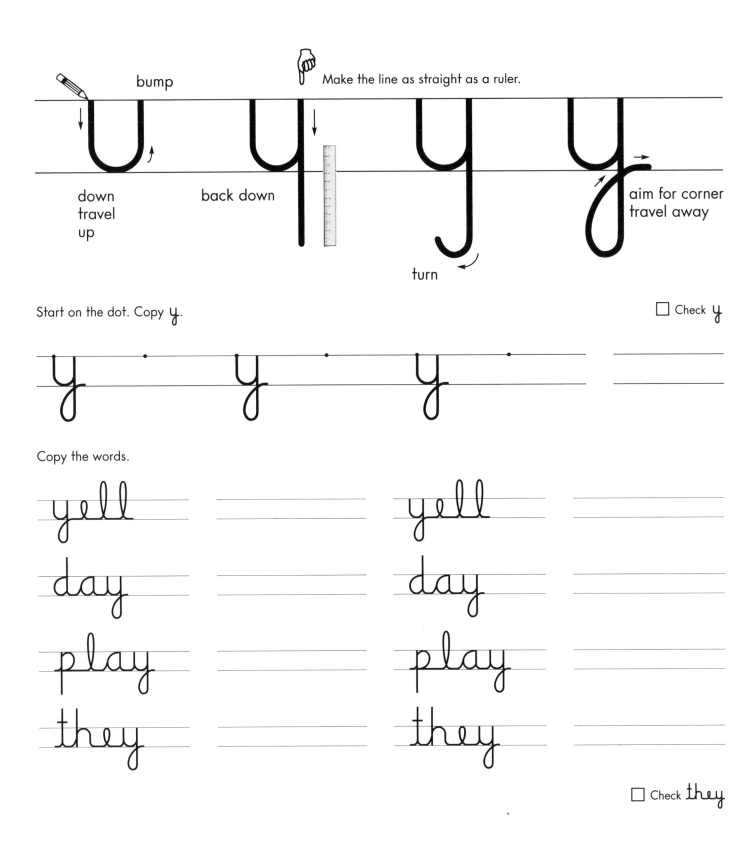

bump

Make the line as straight as a ruler.

down
travel
up

back down

turn

aim for corner
travel away

Start on the dot. Copy y.

☐ Check y

y   y   y

Copy the words.

yell   yell

day   day

play   play

they   they

☐ Check they

Copy y.

y   y   y   y   y

90° →

Add ty.

twenty   six

thir   seven

fort   eigh

fif   nine

Copy the sentences.

Yul   yelled,   "Help!"

Y   H

Yul   played   all   day.

Y

☐ Check Sentence

Cursive Handwriting   **31**

i is i

Seeing spots?
No, these are dots.

dot

bump

travel up

back down
bump
travel away

Start on the dot. Copy i.

☐ Check i

i . i . i .

Copy the words.

it   it

idea   idea

high   high

itch   itch

☐ Check itch

Copy i.

i . i . i . i . i

Add ill.

spill
ch
f
thr

Add it.

exit
kn
spl
sk

Add ip.

ship
cl
dr
tr

Copy the sentences.

Ida pitched it high.

I

Ida did a high flip.

I

☐ Check Sentence

j is *j*

Seeing spots?
No, these are dots.

• dot

bump

travel
up

back
down

turn

aim for corner
travel away

Start on the dot. Copy *j*.

☐ Check *j*

Copy the words.

jelly

jelly

jet

jet

juicy

juicy

jug

jug

☐ Check *jug*

Copy *j*.

j . j . j . j . j

Copy the words.

jay   jay

judge   judge

jeep   jeep

eject   eject

Copy the sentences.

Jade ate a juicy peach.

J

Jaylee juggled.

J

☐ Check Sentence

a b c d e f g h i j k l m

m o p q r s t u v w x y z

Cursive with new letters: u y i j

Wait for the teacher to play The Freeze Game.

jeep - deep   pay - jay

fight - tight   life - lift

jet - get   field - yield

full - pull   itch - pitch

Print to Cursive	Spelling to Cursive

dig → dig

guy, g-u-y

Here are irregular verbs.
Translate print into cursive.

Wait for the teacher to spell the words.
Write the Silly Spelling Words in cursive.

1. dig

2. dug

3. pay

4. paid

5. catch

6. caught

7. light

8. lit

1. _____

2. _____

3. _____

4. _____

5. _____

6. _____

7. _____

8. _____

See teacher's guide.   *Cursive Handwriting* **37**

k is **k**

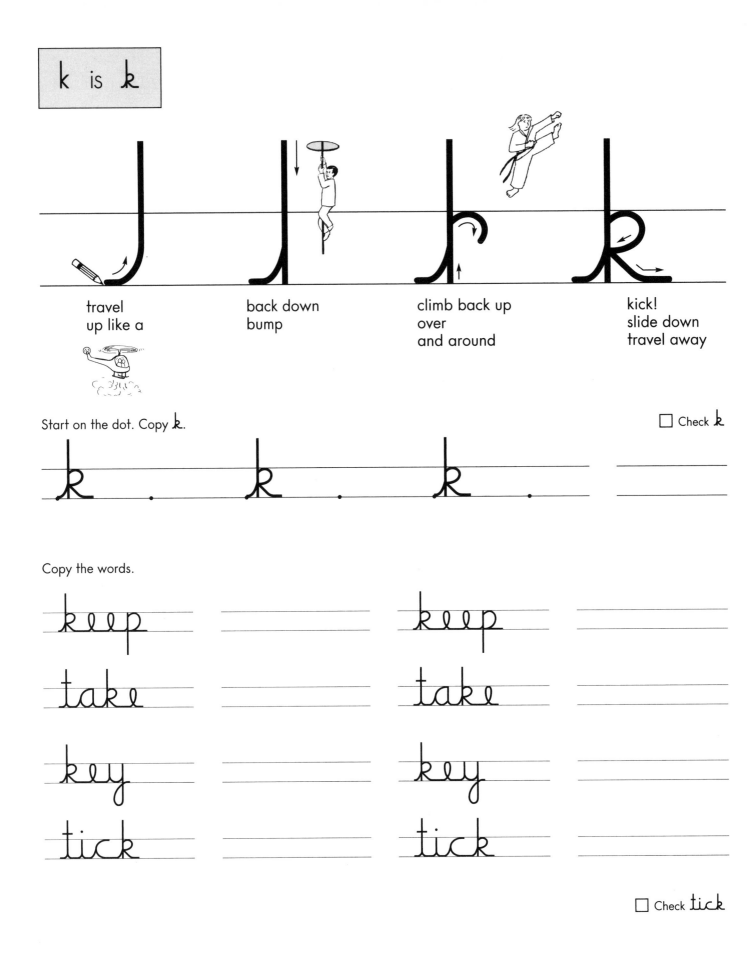

travel
up like a

back down
bump

climb back up
over
and around

kick!
slide down
travel away

Start on the dot. Copy k. ☐ Check k

k   .   k   .   k   .   _____

Copy the words.

keep _____ keep _____

take _____ take _____

key _____ key _____

tick _____ tick _____

☐ Check tick

Copy k.

k . k . k . k . k

Add ick.

trick

br

th

st

Add kle.

pickle

tic

wrin

am

Copy the sentences.

Keith kept the key.

K

Kelly flipped the kayak.

K

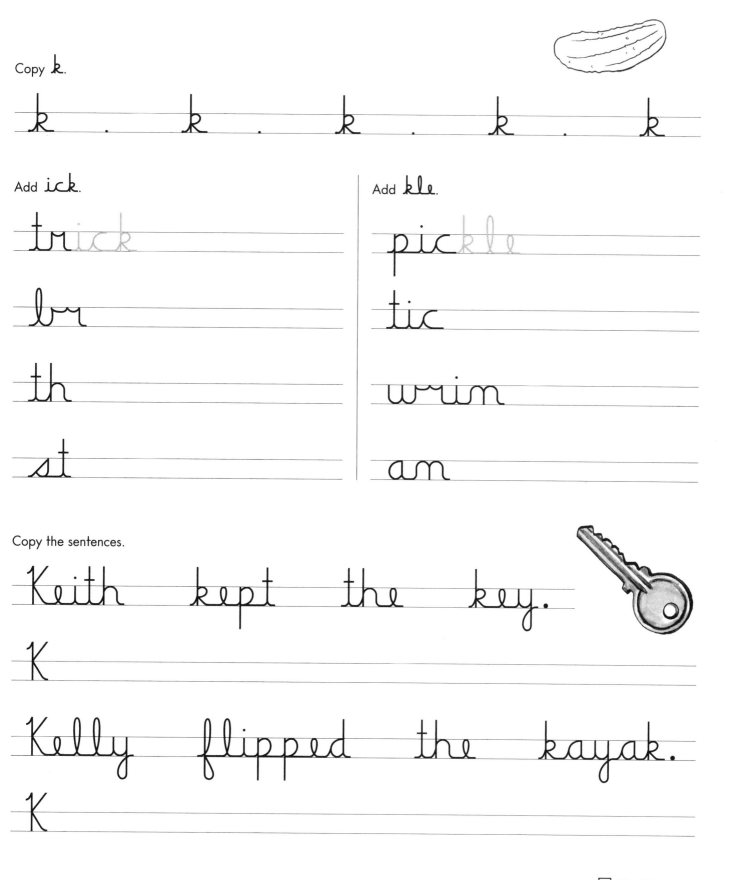

☐ Check Sentence

r is ꓣ

bump

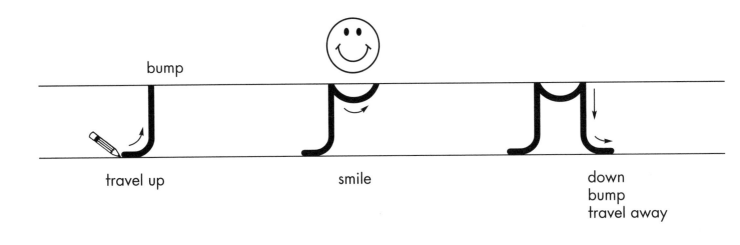

travel up   smile   down
bump
travel away

Start on the dot. Copy ꓣ.   ☐ Check ꓣ

ꓣ .   ꓣ .   ꓣ .   _____

Copy the words.

race   _____   race   _____

are   _____   are   _____

after   _____   after   _____

their   _____   their   _____

☐ Check *their*

Copy M.

M . M . M . M . M

Add ere.

where

th

h

sph

Add ear.

Dear

m

y

f

Add ar.

star

c

f

j

Copy the sentences.

Rafael placed third.

R

Rafael raced after her.

R

☐ Check Sentence

s is ♫

First make a straight jet takeoff!

bump

straight jet takeoff

down
make a J-turn

bump
travel away

Start on the dot. Copy ♫.

☐ Check ♫

Copy the words.

she   she

ship   ship

kiss   kiss

rust   rust

☐ Check rust

© 2018 Learning Without Tears

Copy _A._

_A . A . A . A . A . A . A_

Add _est._

tall_est_

short

hard

soft

Add _ist._

art_ist_

dent

flor

styl

Copy the sentences.

Sarah skates fast.

_S_

Seth tells tall tales.

_S_

☐ Check Sentence

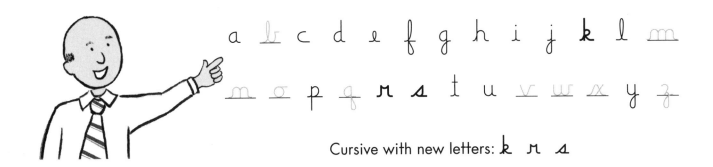

a b c d e f g h i j k l m
m o p q r s t u v w x y z

Cursive with new letters: k r s

Wait for the teacher to play The Freeze Game.

she - her   kid - rid

pair - fair   pick - trick

just - rust   ace - aces

rake - take   paid - raid

risk, r-i-s-k

sit → sit

Here are irregular verbs.
Translate print into cursive.

Wait for the teacher to spell the words.
Write the Silly Spelling Words in cursive.

1. sit _____   _____   1. _____

2. sat _____   _____   2. _____

3. keep _____   _____   3. _____

4. kept _____   _____   4. _____

5. say _____   _____   5. _____

6. said _____   _____   6. _____

7. read _____   _____   7. _____

8. read _____   _____   8. _____

o is *o*

Now you are ready to learn the Tow Truck Letters. Tow Truck Letters always end with a tow.

tow →

Magic c   keep on   bump   end with a tow
                 going

Start on the dot. Copy *o*.   ☐ Check *o*

Copy the words.

out   *out*

oar   *oar*

coat   *coat*

loud   *loud*

☐ Check *loud*

Copy o.

o　　　o　　　o　　　o　　　o

Add our.

four
p
y
h

Add oat.

boat
c
fl
g

Add ock.

lock
d
sh
bl

Copy the sentences.

Otto plays soccer.

O

Octopuses grasp prey.

O

☐ Check Sentence

w is **ш**

Tow Truck Letters always end with a tow.

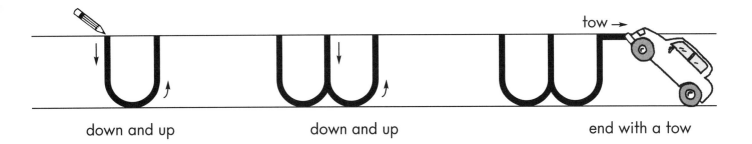

tow →

down and up   down and up   end with a tow

Start on the dot. Copy **ш**.   ☐ Check **ш**

Copy the words.

ша   **ша**

claш   **claш**

wash   **wash**

jaш   **jaш**

☐ Check **jaш**

Copy w.

w   w   w   w   w

Add way.

subway

free

jet

high

Add low.

pillow

hol

yel

fol

Copy the sentences.

Willy   saw   the   walrus.

W

Wait,   oh,   please   wait!

W

☐ Check Sentence

b is **ℓ**

Tow Truck Letters always end with a tow.

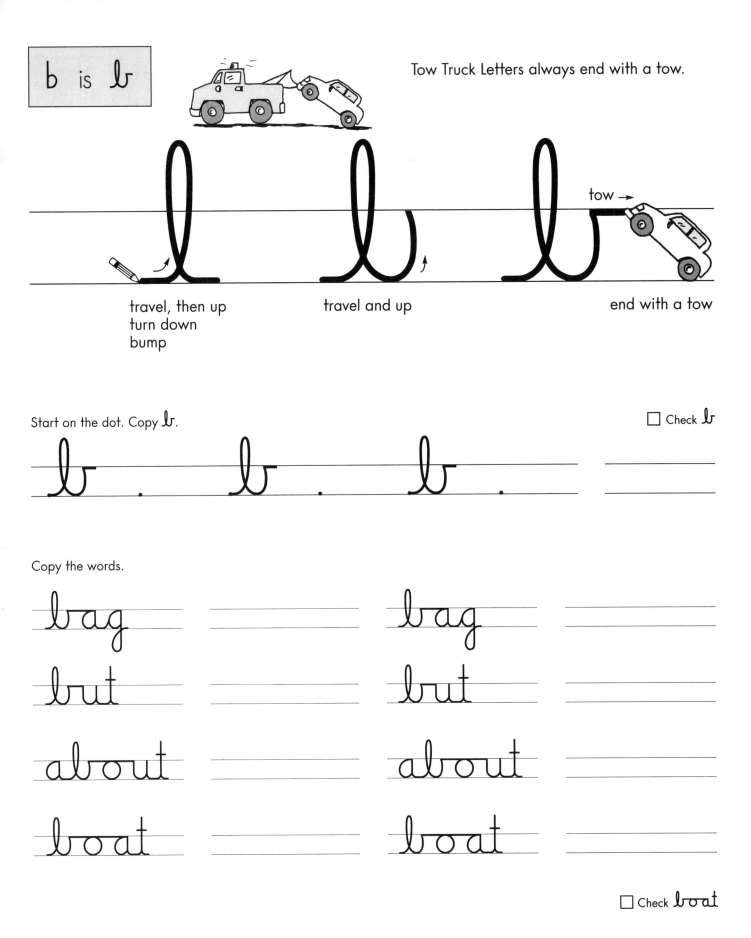

travel, then up
turn down
bump

travel and up

tow →

end with a tow

Start on the dot. Copy **ℓ**.

☐ Check **ℓ**

ℓ . ℓ . ℓ . _____

Copy the words.

bag		bag	
but		but	
about		about	
boat		boat	

☐ Check **boat**

Copy b.

b . b . b . b . b

Copy the words.

baby   baby

crab   crab

base   base

bugs   bugs

Copy the sentences.

Bats fly out at dusk.

B

Bats eat little bugs.

B

☐ Check Sentence

v	is	⋁

Tow Truck Letters always end with a tow.

tow →

slide down   and up   end with a tow

Start on the dot. Copy ⋁.

Copy the words.

vow   vow

vast   vast

lava   lava

value   value

Copy V.

V V V V V

Copy the words.

vase   vase

vary   vary

vocal   vocal

vault   vault

Copy the sentences.

Vultures are bald.

V

Vipers are reptiles.

V

☐ Check Sentence

Tricky Connections – after o

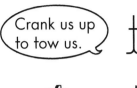

t   k   l   f

t   k   l   f

Copy the models.

hot   took   old   of

big smile
for the tow

i   n   e   s

i   n   e   s

Copy the models.

oil   or   toe   lost

54 *Cursive Handwriting*   © 2018 Learning Without Tears

Tricky Connections – after ꞈ

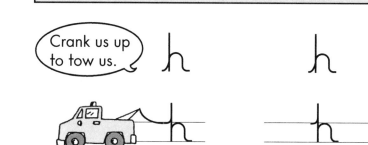

h   h   h   h

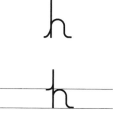

h   h   h   h

Copy the models.

who   what   where   why

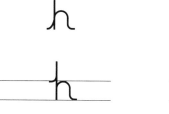

big smile
for the tow

i   n   l   s

 i   n   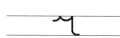 e   s

Copy the models.

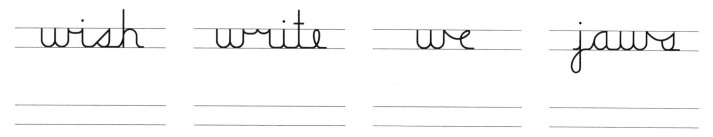

wish   write   we   jaws

Tricky Connections – after b

 Crank us up to tow us.   l   l   b   b

 l   l   b   b

Copy the models.

blue   *black*   *rabbit*   *tabby*

big smile
for the tow

 Crank us up to tow us.   i   n   e   s

 i   n   e   s

Copy the models.

bite   *brag*   *best*   *tubs*

Tricky Connections – after ∨

big smile
for the tow

Crank us up
to tow us.

ℓ   ℓ   ℓ   ℓ

e   e   e   e

Copy the models.

very   verb   save   have

Crank us up
to tow us.

i   i   i   i

i   i   i   i

Copy the models.

vice   video   view   virus

a b c d e f g h i j k l m

m o p q r s t u v w x y z

Cursive with new letters: b o v w

Wait for the teacher to play The Freeze Game.

what - where

for - before

over - ever

avid - avoid

hot - got

best - vest

blue - value

look - took

See teacher's guide.

bow, b-o-w

Here are irregular verbs.
Translate print into cursive.

Wait for the teacher to spell the words.
Write the Silly Spelling Words in cursive.

1. lose

2. lost

3. give

4. gave

5. write

6. wrote

7. buy

8. bought

1.

2.

3.

4.

5.

6.

7.

8.

m is m

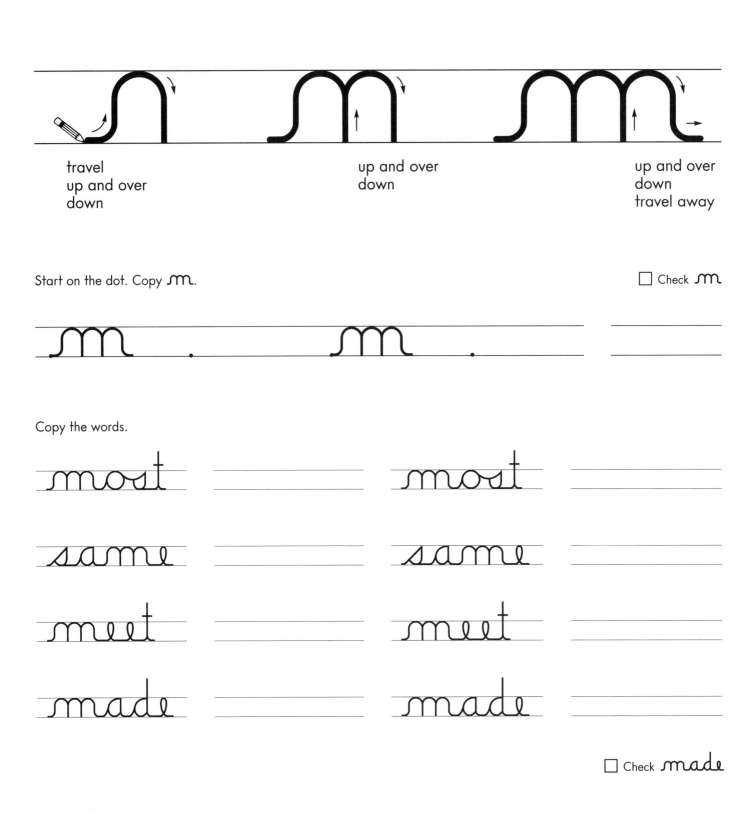

travel
up and over
down

up and over
down

up and over
down
travel away

Start on the dot. Copy m.

☐ Check m

m .   m .

Copy the words.

most   most

same   same

meet   meet

made   made

☐ Check made

© 2018 Learning Without Tears

Copy _m_.

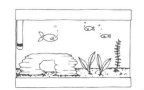

_m_ . _m_ . _m_ . _m_ . _m_

Add _ium_.

calcium   aquar

uran   stad

sod   med

lith   gymnas

Copy the sentences.

Some mammals swim.

S

Mice are mammals.

m

☐ Check Sentence

n is ⌢

travel
up and over
down

up and over
down
travel away

Start on the dot. Copy m.

☐ Check m

m.   m.   m.

Copy the words.

mot   mot

and   and

near   near

mail   mail

☐ Check mail

© 2018 Learning Without Tears

Copy m.

m. m. m. m. m.

Copy the words.

nest   nest

nose   nose

even   even

name   name

Copy the sentences.

Saturn has many rings.

S

Neptune is a planet.

N

☐ Check Sentence

SPECIAL SITUATION

After a Tow Truck Letter, use **printed** m.

Start on the dot. Copy m. ☐ Check m

m · m ·

come   come

from   from

home   home

some   some

☐ Check some

SPECIAL SITUATION

After a Tow Truck Letter, use **printed** n.

Start on the dot. Copy n.   ☐ Check n

n   n   n

Copy the words.

on   on

own   own

only   only

more   more

☐ Check more

x is ⅄x or x

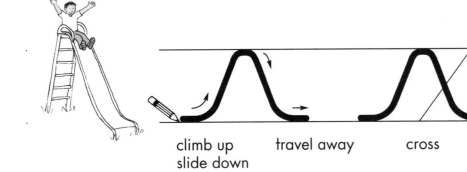

Don't cross me until you finish writing the word.

x

climb up
slide down

travel away

cross

after σ
slide down
cross

Start on the dot. Copy x.

☐ Check x

x .   x .   x .

Copy the words.

exit _____ exit _____

sixty _____ sixty _____

tax _____ tax _____

exam _____ exam _____

☐ Check exam

Copy _x_ and _x_.

_x_ . _x_ . _x_ . _x_ . _x_

Add _ix_.

mix

f

s

m

Add _ox_.

fox

b

phl

l

Copy the sentences.

X-rays show bones.

X

Xavier took an exam.

X

☐ Check Sentence

Cursive Handwriting **67**

q is q

Here's how to make c into q.

bump

Magic c

up like a

back down

U-turn

aim for corner
travel away

Start on the dot. Copy q.

q ·   q ·   q ·

Copy the words.

☐ Check q

quiet   quick   equal   queen

Copy the sentence.

☐ Check queen

Quinn wrote the quote.

Q

☐ Check Sentence

z is ʒ

Here's a heart.

My half   Your half

make your half

start another half down

aim for corner travel away

turn

Start on the dot. Copy ʒ.

ʒ   ʒ   ʒ

Copy the words.   ☐ Check ʒ

zoom   zebra   size   dozen

Copy the sentence.   ☐ Check dozen

Zoe picked zinnias.

ʒ

☐ Check Sentence

Review & Mastery: Cursive to Cursive

a b c d e f g h i j k l m
n o p q r s t u v w x y z

Cursive with new letters: m n q x z

Wait for the teacher to play The Freeze Game.

came - same   come - some

win - mine   won - none

six - fix   box - fox

quit - quiz   size - prize

See teacher's guide.

Print to Cursive	Spelling to Cursive

quiz, q-u-i-z

make → make

Here are the irregular verbs.
Translate print into cursive.

Wait for the teacher to spell the words.
Write the Silly Spelling Words in cursive.

1. make

2. made

3. know

4. knew

5. freeze

6. froze

7. quit

8. quit

1.

2.

3.

4.

5.

6.

7.

8.

See teacher's guide.   *Cursive Handwriting*

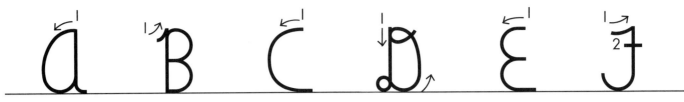

Trace the steps.

Trace the first word. Copy the sentences.

C a a

Magic C   up   back down

Al asked, "Are you asleep?"

1 P B

ready down   up around   around again

Bob backpacked in Brazil.

C

Magic C

Cindy called Cousin Carl.

1 d D

down small turn   flip over   curve up end

Dan drove on Delo Dr.

C E

c in the air   c again

Ed enjoyed Europe.

1 J J

ready down   J-turn   cross

Fiona flew on Friday.

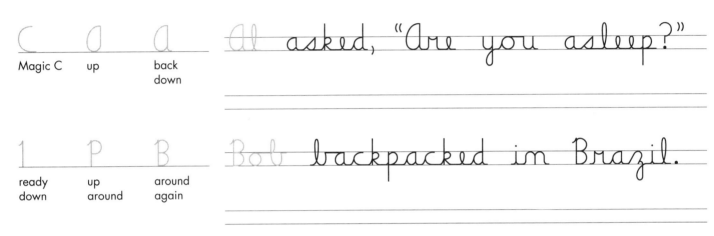

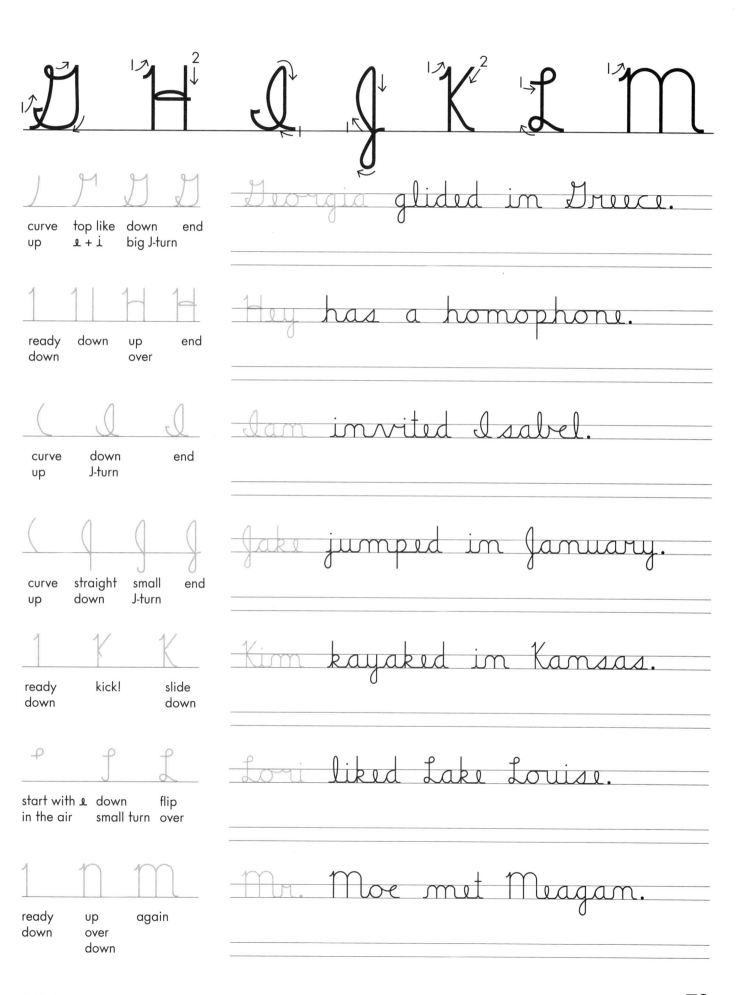

G

curve up — top like ℓ + i — down big J-turn — end

Georgia glided in Greece.

H

ready down — down — up over — end

Hey has a homophone.

I

curve up — down J-turn — end

Iam invited Isabel.

J

curve up — straight down — small J-turn — end

Jake jumped in January.

K

ready down — kick! — slide down

Kim kayaked in Kansas.

L

start with ℓ in the air — down small turn — flip over

Lori liked Lake Louise.

M

ready down — up over down — again

Mr. Moe met Meagan.

N O P 2 R S J

1 n
ready down / up over down

Nov. is for November.

C O O
Magic C / keep on going / end

Ottawa is in Ontario.

1 P
ready down / up around

Pre- is a prefix.

Q or 2 2 2
half heart / small turn / flip over

Quit that, Quentin!

1 P R
ready down / up around / slide down

Raisa reads Russian.

/ S S
straight jet takeoff / print S / end

Sue signed, "Sincerely, Sue."

1 J
ready down / J-turn

Today isn't Thanksgiving.

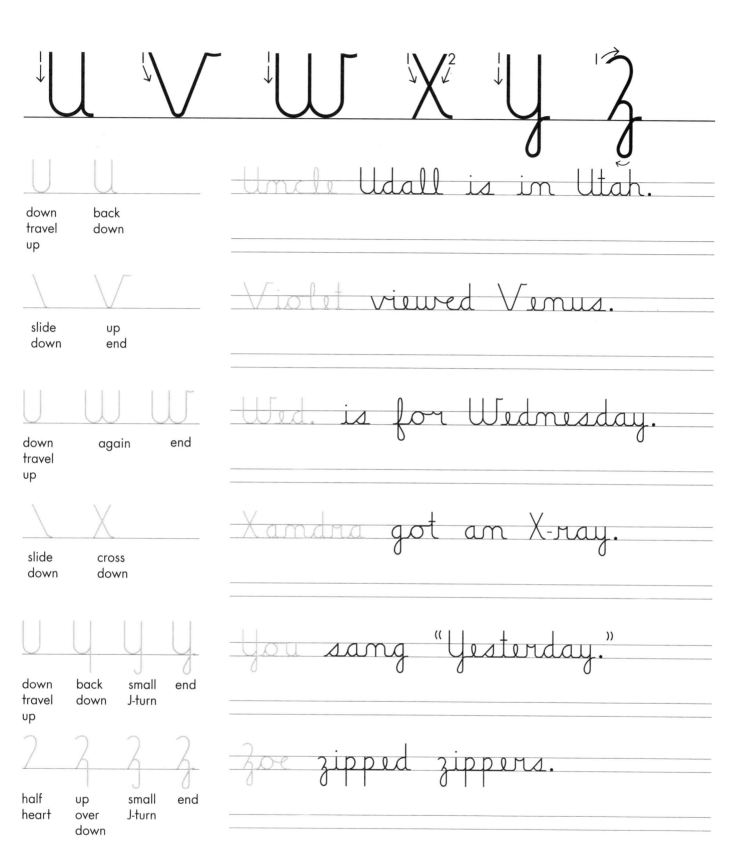

U
down
travel
up

U
back
down

Uncle Udall is in Utah.

V
slide
down

V
up
end

Violet viewed Venus.

U
down
travel
up

W
again

W
end

Wed. is for Wednesday.

X
slide
down

X
cross
down

Xandra got an X-ray.

U
down
travel
up

Y
back
down

Y
small
J-turn

Y
end

You sang "Yesterday."

Z
half
heart

Z
up
over
down

Z
small
J-turn

Z
end

Zoe zipped zippers.

CAPITAL CONNECTIONS

These capitals connect. Copy the capitals and connect to the lowercase letter.

Aa   Cc   Ee   Jj   Kk   Ll   Mm

Nn   Qq   Rr   Uu   Yy   Zz

These capitals DO NOT connect. Copy.

Bb   Dd   Ff   Gg   Hh   Ii   Oo

Pp   Ss   Tt   Vv   Ww   Xx

CAPITAL REVIEW

Translate the capitals into cursive.

A   B   C   D   E   F   G   H

I   J   K   L   M   N   O   P   Q

R   S   T   U   V   W   X   Y   Z

POEM

You're or Your?

If you're (you are) going for a run,

You're, the contraction, is the one,

But if you have lost your shoes,

Possessive your is what to use.

Change print to cursive.

We're racing for our team.

WORDS

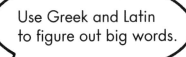

Use Greek and Latin to figure out big words.

Copy.
PREFIXES

pre- = before

preview

auto- = self

autograph

WORD ROOTS

aqua = water

aquarium

graph = writing

geography

geo, terra = earth

territory

SUFFIXES

-arium = place for

terrarium

-ology = study of

geology

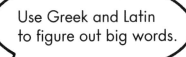

PARAGRAPH

Political Map North America

Greenland

Canada

United States of America

Cuba

Mexico

Costa Rica

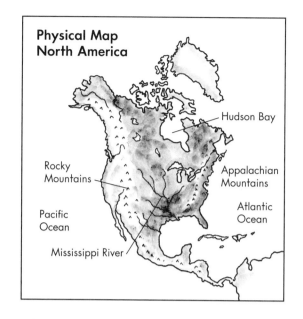

Physical Map North America

Hudson Bay

Rocky Mountains

Appalachian Mountains

Pacific Ocean

Atlantic Ocean

Mississippi River

POLITICAL MAPS
Land and water outlines
Countries – names and borders

PHYSICAL MAPS
Land – terrain: mountains, deserts, flat lands
Water features – rivers, lakes

Use the information. Complete the body of the paragraph.

Look at maps. All maps are flat.

Political maps show

Physical maps show

Maps show different things.

PUNCTUATION

Copy the punctuation marks.

. _ . _ . _ . _ . _ . _   ? _ ? _ ? _   ! _ ! _ ! _

Periods   Question marks   Exclamation points

DATES

Here are the birth dates of important people.
Some of them are in this book. Copy the dates.

Jan. 11, 1755   Feb. 15, 1820   Mar. 4, 1877

Apr. 25, 1917   May 3, 1919   June 5, 1899

July 29, 1877   Aug. 5, 1930   Sept. 26, 1898

Oct. 2, 1869   Nov. 30, 1835   Dec. 25, 1821

GREETINGS & CLOSINGS

☐ Check Word

Copy.

Dear   Sincerely,   Thank you,   Love,

FRIENDLY LETTER

Write a thank you letter. Organize your letter like this.

Date
Month Day, Year

Greeting
Dear _____ ,

Body
Say, "thank you" and explain how much you appreciate the gift or help. Mention what it is or what they did. Add details to make it more personal.

Use a comma:
1. After the day of the month
2. After the greeting
3. After the closing

Closing
Sincerely, Thank you, or Love,

Signature

WORDS

astronomer   author   inventor   pianist   magician   philosopher   jazz singer

These are suffixes for people: – er, – or, – ist, – ian.

Copy.

– er: astronomer, diver, teacher

– or: author, doctor, inventor

– ist: pianist, dentist, motorist

– ian: magician, physician, optician

– er: philosopher, jazz singer

– ist: scientist, artist

PARAGRAPH

Galileo

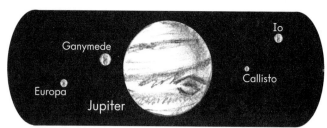

Ganymede   Io

Europa   Callisto

Jupiter

Look at the night sky. If

it's clear, you'll see countless stars,

a few planets, and one moon.

Galileo, an astronomer, was the

first to see more moons. In 1609,

he made a telescope strong enough

to see four of Jupiter's moons.

SYMBOLS

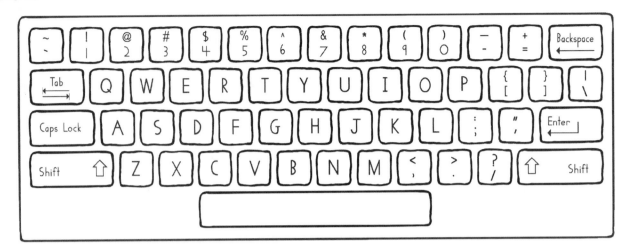

1. exclamation	6. caret
2. at	7. and
3. number	8. asterisk
4. dollar	9. open parenthesis
5. percent	0. close parenthesis

Write the symbol name in cursive.

! _____   ^ _____

@ _____   & _____

_____   * _____

$ _____   (_____

% _____   ) _____

LETTERS

Shh!
Silent letters

knack   knife   knew   knees

wreck   wrap   write   wrist

climb   lamb   crumb   thumb

Write sentences with some of the words.

SENTENCES

Capitalize titles like: Mr., Dr., Ms., Miss, Mrs.
Capitalize the first, last, and important words in book, movie, and song titles.

CAPITALIZE:	Finish the sentences about yourself.
Schools	*My school is* _____.
Titles, names	*My teacher is* _____.
Book titles	*I read* _____.
Movie titles	*I saw* _____.
Song titles	*I can sing* _____.
Cities, towns	*I live in* _____.
Rivers, lakes, oceans	*The closest water is* _____.
First word of a quote	*I said,* " _____ ".

☐ Check Sentence

NAMES
Copy the names.

- Born Sept. 26, 1898
- Pianist and composer
- Wrote "Rhapsody in Blue"

George Gershwin

- Born April 29, 1899
- Composer, pianist, and bandleader
- Wrote "It Don't Mean a Thing"

Duke Ellington

- Born April 25, 1917
- Jazz singer and "First Lady of Song"
- Sang "I've Got Rhythm"

Ella Fitzgerald

- Born May 3, 1919
- Folk singer and composer
- Wrote "If I Had a Hammer"

Pete Seeger

Write about one of these musicians or another favorite of yours.

PARAGRAPH

TROPICAL RAINFOREST

EMERGENT LAYER: parrots, butterflies

CANOPY: monkeys, toucans

UNDERSTORY: sloths, snakes, lizards

FOREST FLOOR: insects, jaguars, anteaters, frogs

Finish the sentences.

A tropical rainforest bursts with life. At the top,

Just below

The understory

The floor is home to

© 2018 Learning Without Tears

SENTENCES

CAPITALIZE: Finish the sentences about yourself.

Initials

My initials are __ . __ . __ .

Names

My name is

Days

Today is

Months

My birthday is in

Languages

I speak

Holidays

My favorite holiday is

Names

I admire

Places

I would like to visit

☐ Check Sentence

PARAGRAPH

sponge

Garret Augustus Morgan, Sr.
born March 4, 1877
inventor of safety hood device
1916 Lake Erie tunnel explosion

Men were trapped

in the smoky tunnel.

Firemen couldn't go in.

Then, Garret put on his safety

hood invention. A wet sponge

cooled and cleaned the air. He

could breathe! He saved two lives.

☐ Check Sentences

WORDS

Fill in the blanks to make compound words.

sun   _sun_   +   _light_   =   _sunlight_

rain   _____   +   _bow_   =   _____

fire   _____   +   _fly_   =   _____

lantern   _____   +   _fish_   =   _____

bed   _____   +   _time_   =   _____

SIX SYL – LA – BLE WORD

bi – o – lu – mi – nes – cent

bio   _biolumi_   _bioluminescent_

PARAGRAPH

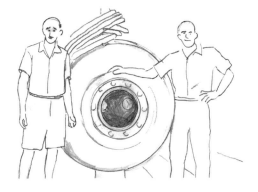

Bathysphere
- Strong, steel hollow ball
- Tied to ship, lowered and raised
- Oxygen hoses, phone, and electric cables
- 1930–1934 near Bermuda

Bathysphere

William Beebe, born July 25, 1877
- Planned dive to deep ocean (Abyss)
- Marine biologist, famous scientist
- First to see the Abyss with Barton
- Described bioluminescent creatures

Otis Barton, born June 5, 1899
- Heard about Beebe's plan
- Engineer with design ideas
- Inventor of Bathysphere
- Made deepest dive with Beebe

Finish the paragraph.

Beebe and Barton were a team.

PARAGRAPH

What's in the midnight zone,

the deep, dark ocean? There's

a light show! Bioluminescent

animals glow and blink.

SENTENCES

Always do right.

Mark Twain
- Born Nov. 30, 1835

Translate the quotations into cursive.

Mark Twain said, "Always do right."

Independence is happiness.

Susan B. Anthony
- Born Feb. 15, 1820

学而时习之，不亦说乎.

To learn and to practice is a joy.

Confucius
- Born Sept. 28, 551 BCE

☐ Check Sentence